The Watchers

Dedication

To my children, grandchildren, great-grandchildren and those yet to come, this story is specially for you.

Enjoy!

Copyright © Anita Lucas 2016

The Watchers

by

Anita Lucas

2016

Contents

The Meeting	Page 1
The Supervisor	Page 07
The Dream	Page 15
Granny Green	Page 22
A Plan	Page 35
Getting Help	Page 48
Caught	Page 53
Max and Joseph	Page 61
The Police Station	Page 63
The Landlord	Page 68
Rewards	Page 71

The Meeting

All was not well on Green Street. The mutterings and moanings had gone on all night. The chimney pots almost glowed as hot as the fires below them, sending thick black smoke billowing up into the sky. Never before had there been such a panic. Ideas were suggested and thrown out. Tempers were lost and tears shed - something that had never happened before. It was disastrous. What was to be done? Such was the commotion that house windows below had been pushed open. Sleepy heads had peered out. Then windows had slammed shut again. Curtains fluttered and lights went on and off, up and down the street.

Finally, up above, a decision was taken. Someone must go to the Command Centre and speak with the Supervisor. He would know what to do. Within minutes a bag was produced, it contained pieces of folded paper; one piece for each person. Only one paper would have a cross on it.

The person who drew that piece of paper would be the one to go and speak to the Supervisor.

Worried faces stared intently at the bag. The Supervisor at Command Centre was very important. He became very cross if anyone was silly. He didn't like to be disturbed when he had a lot of important jobs to do. Still, this was very important too. A hand went into the bag and pulled out a piece of folded paper, and then another and another until everyone held a paper in their hand. Someone counted -one - two - three - and everyone opened their piece of paper. All but one breathed a sigh of relief. Their papers were blank. Everyone looked around waiting to see who did have the paper with the cross on it.

"It's me," said a quiet voice. "I'll go straight away. The rest of you can go home to your houses and tomorrow I'll let you know what the Supervisor had to say."

"Look," said a voice from the back, "if you're scared I'll go with you." Two bright shiny blue eyes looked into the eyes of the person with the paper. "And my friend will come too. You might need help."

"May be so," said the girl with the crossed paper "although I'll be lucky if I actually get to see the secretary, let alone speak to the Supervisor. Still, I suppose three's better than one even if we don't manage to say anything. I've heard that the Supervisor can be a bit, a bit – err,"

"Frightening?" suggested her new friend. "Well, yeah, he did sort out those boys, Lee and Len, who were breaking windows in Green Street. Gave them a real fright he did. I heard he slammed the door of a house just as they were throwing the bricks. It frightened the life out of them because they thought that the houses were empty. They've not been back since – at least not 'til now."

"Well, "she said, "they might have run away that time but we know they are back again. They're trouble. Still, I suppose if the Supervisor did that, he must be scary. Look, if you really want to come along I don't suppose it will do any harm. What did you say your names were?"

"I'm Billy Blue Wings," he said. "Billy for short and my friend here is Sammy Sunshine or just Sammy."

"Hello," said Sammy. His eyes were brown and he had the most beautiful golden yellow wings which were beating so fast they kept knocking off his yellow cap. Billy picked up the offending cap and rammed it hard on Sammy's head, covering his eyes.

"I can't see," moaned Sammy.

"Then use your eyes to peer through the holes, and you'd better tuck away your wings!" muttered Billy. *His* blue wings were tucked neatly behind his back and his blue striped scarf was wrapped around them. He turned to look at her. "You're Rosy Red Wings, aren't you?" "Yes," she said stretching her red wings out to show him. The wings were covered in beautiful red spots.

"Don't think I've seen you around here before," said Sammy, "at least, not until tonight."

"That's because I only moved here a while ago," Rosy replied. "I lived in Green Street where those boys are messing about but the house was supposedly condemned so my girl and her parents had to move out. Those boys were probably trying to break in trying to see if there was anything to steal. That's why I had to get help. I think that's when the Supervisor came to sort things out."

"Yes, but how did you know what the boys were doing if you had moved here?" said Billy.

"Because I was still there in Green Street," said Rosy.

"But you just said you had moved here when the family moved," puzzled Billy.

"Well, you only stay with a family if they go on believing in you. Mine never really got started. Just as my girl was old enough to understand about Watchers, they moved out, so I didn't have time to move with them. However, now that I've found out where my girl lives, I'll be able to introduce myself. That's why I'm here tonight."

"What's she like?" asked Billy. "Does she know about Watchers?"

"I don't know yet," answered Rosy. "I'm hoping she's heard about Guardian Angels – that's what grownups call us. It will make explaining much easier. She'll probably be a bit frightened at first. If she's not a believer then I'm out of a job and could be sent away - banished!" A tear glistened on Rosy's eyelash. "Anyway, let's get going. We've a lot to do tonight! Those boys are still trouble and who knows what they'll be up to next."

The Supervisor

The Supervisor's office was a short way away from the meeting place. It was on the top of a tall office block. The roof was flat with a small hatchway leading into the building. A wire mesh gate was attached to the side of the hatchway. Two Watchers were standing at the side of the hatchway keeping guard. The three new friends landed on the roof and folded back their wings.

"Careful where you put your feet," said Rosy. "The pigeons here don't worry about leaving poo blobs around and they can really mess up your shoes. I don't think the Supervisor would be pleased to have us leaving sticky footprints all over his floor."

"Yuk!" groaned Billy as he narrowly missed stepping on a large grey sloppy puddle in front of him.

"Disgusting!" groaned Sammy as he wiped the bottom of his trainers across a clean part of the roof surface.

The two guards watched the three friends walk towards them. "What do you want?" asked the taller of the two.

"Err – we need to talk to the Supervisor," stammered Rosy.

"Yeah," joined in Billy as he eyed the large club that the guard was holding in front of them, "and we need to see him quickly. There's trouble at Green Street."

"Green Street?" repeated the guard. "Is that the same Green Street where those two guys were messing about recently, in those old houses?"

"Yes," nodded Billy, "and they haven't learned their lesson. They are still breaking into them."

"O.K." said the guard. "Follow me!"

He led the way through a gap in the wire cage and squeezed through a ventilator in the wall. A metal duct attached to the ventilator led straight into a large room. Each wall had a ventilator similar to the one they had climbed through. In the centre of the room was a table. It was made from a large take-away carton and was covered in papers. Three people were around the table sitting on upturned yoghurt pots. One of the people was writing on a roll of paper; one was reading from another paper roll, whilst the third, the Supervisor, was sitting between them listening carefully and nodding his head. He was wearing a very smart black overall with a badge on the pocket showing a large 'S'. His hair was grey and matched his grey beard. The three friends waited quietly in front of the table. Sammy and Billy looked nervously at each other. Rosy softly cleared her throat.

"Excuse me, sir," she said politely, "could we have a word with you?"

The Supervisor turned and stared at Rosy. Rosy felt herself shaking. She held her breath.

"Well now," said the Supervisor, his face suddenly breaking into a warm smile. "How can I help you?"

Plucking up her courage, she began, "My name is Rosy Red Wings" and she began to tell him about the meeting and how she had been chosen to come and see him.

"I'm pleased to meet you Rosy," he said, "and who are these two people?"

"Oh! We've just met, at the meeting, that is. They said they'd come with me to – err – err,"

"To protect you from me?" he asked.

"Well, well – y - yes," stuttered Rosy. "This is Billy Blue Wings and this is Sammy Sunshine."

A smile spread across the Supervisor's face. "Don't worry. I won't eat you up. Let me see – Billy Blue Wings – you belong to Max, or at least you will do soon."

Billy looked surprised.

"And you, young man" he continued, looking at Sammy, "You will soon belong to Joe."

Sammy's mouth opened to speak but nothing came out.

"Rosy – Rosy - let me think," the Supervisor puzzled. "Now, who do you belong to?"

"Err, well, I'm supposed to belong to the girl Lily who lived in Green Street, but she's had to move, and no one else came to live in the house, so I went to find her, but she's only just old enough to know about Watchers and, and,"

"Stop," said the Supervisor gently. "Calm down, and tell me what's happening over there."

"Well, it's those boys you sorted out a few weeks ago. I think they're called Lee and Len. They're at it again, causing bother I mean," blurted out Sammy.

"I see," said the Supervisor. "Well, I'm sure we can keep a look out for them."

"No!" shouted Rosy. "That's not what we REALLY came for!"

Sammy and Billy looked at each other. Rosy had actually – shouted – at the Supervisor.

He turned towards Rosy.

"Well, I hope this is not going to take too long because I'm very busy!"

"Sorry. I didn't mean to shout at you," said Rosy remembering her manners, "but you see, all the houses in Green Street are empty except one. The landlord has thrown out the people, telling them the houses are condemned and going to be pulled down. He really wants to sell the land for a lot of money. He doesn't care about the families who have made a home there. A lot of our Watchers have lost their families because they've moved away and it could be a long time before new houses are built. In fact, there might not be any. They might build a factory, or a car park and then YOU would have an awful lot of extra work on your hands and-"

Rosy stopped. She'd run out of things to say. The room was very quiet. The Supervisor was pulling his beard and staring at the table top. Rosy looked at him. Was he angry or just thinking? Minutes went by. No one moved. The Supervisor cleared his throat and looked up.

"Right," he informed them. "I want you to go away. Go back to the other Watchers and tell them this. At the moment I am very busy sorting out new homes for the Watchers on Primrose Hill who have all been without families since their old houses collapsed. It's an emergency I must deal with first. My Secretary will write down your problems and we will see to them as soon as we can. In the meantime, you must all go to your children and ask them to help."

"How?" asked Billy. "What can children do to help?"

"They must persuade their parents to go to the police, or the Council, or to a lawyer for advice," he answered.

"But – but," stammered Rosy.

"Goodbye!" said the Supervisor, looking away. He nodded to the guard, who escorted them back to the roof.

The Dream

Lily opened one eye, the eye that was poking out of the top of her duvet. It wasn't that she was scared of the dark; it was just that on certain nights the moonlight shone very brightly through the crack in her curtains and made strange shapes on the wall. She knew there was nothing there; she knew she didn't need to be frightened; she knew that her mum and dad were next door (she could hear her dad snoring) but she couldn't help feeling worried sometimes – especially when the shapes looked like faces – strange faces – and hands with long fingers and even longer nails! She had been asleep; she knew that, so why was her one eye open and looking over the top of her duvet?

Then, she heard if again. A strange rustling noise, or was it a squeak, or, or, was it someone whispering? It had an echo-ey sound to it. It seemed to be coming from the old fireplace.

Lily lived in an old Terrace house. Nowadays, new houses that were built in a row were called

Townhouses. "That's the posh name for them," her mum told her. The difference was, that in her house most of the rooms had a fireplace to keep the house warm, even the bedrooms. New Townhouses had central heating. When they had moved in here, Lily's mum and dad decided not to light fires in the bedrooms because they thought it was dangerous.

Lily moved the duvet so that both of her eyes were peering over the edge. Now she could see better as well as listen. There was definitely a soft whispering sound coming from her fireplace. Should she get out of bed and have a look? Should she sit still and see what happened, or should she shout for mum and dad? Then she noticed two tiny specks of light that looked like tiny eyes staring straight across the room at her. Lily held her breath. The eyes blinked. Lily could barely move. The eyes blinked again. Lily stared, trying not to blink herself in case she missed something.

"Shh!" said a whispering noise. "She's awake. I think she heard us."

"Huh!" said another voice. "If she **didn't** hear us, she has now!"

Lily noticed now that there were three sets of blinking eyes and they were moving. Should she shout for mum and dad? Perhaps she was dreaming. Should she hide under the duvet and hope that they would go away? If she shouted for mum and dad they would tell her she was imagining things, and if she hid under the duvet she wouldn't find out what was happening. At least if she watched, she would have a chance to run or scream if it became scarier. She sat still trying not to move a muscle. The eyes seemed to move with a floating motion. One pair hovered just above her eyes and one pair seemed to float over the lumps at the end of her duvet – right where her feet were. The third pair seemed to be hiding behind the bed post at the end of her bed.

"She's definitely awake," squeaked a tiny voice.

"Oh, oh!" declared the voice from behind the bed post. "What do we do now?"

Lily's eyes opened even wider. Now she could pick out a little shape around each set of eyes. The shape closest to her looked like a little girl dressed all in red – red sweatshirt, red tights, red socks and trainers, with red ribbons to fasten her black hair in two long plaits. The shape at the end of the bed was boy-shaped. He, was all in blue – blue sweatshirt, blue jeans and blue socks and trainers. A blue scarf floated round his neck. His hair was short and fair and he had a tiny blue stud in his left ear. At this point Lily noticed that the third pair of eyes was now hovering next to the blue shape. It was another boy shape, but this one was dressed in yellow and there was a yellow cap on his head. He had it the wrong way round. Then Lily realised why the three shapes appeared to be floating in the air. Each of them had tiny flimsy wings which were moving so fast they looked as if they were hardly moving at all. Plucking up her courage, she whispered "Err, who are you?"

The tiny red girl shot back to the end of the bed. "Shall I answer or shall we go?" she asked the two boys.

"Well," said one of them, "she **is** your girl and she might need our help. Let's try."

The red girl darted back to Lily and hovered in front of her eyes.

"I'm Rosy Red Wings, Rosy for short. These are my friends, Billy Blue Wings and Sammy Sunshine. You're Lily aren't you?"

"How did you know that?" asked Lily. "I've never seen you before."

"Well," answered Rosy, "that's easy. We are here all the time. I belong to your house. In fact I'm your Watcher!"

Lily couldn't believe her ears. Surely she was dreaming? This little person was saying she lived in her house and was her Watcher – her Watcher? "I don't understand. How come I haven't seen you before? Am I dreaming? Is this a trick? I think I'd better get my mum and dad."

"No! Don't do that!" exclaimed Rosy. "We won't hurt you. We're here to give you help and that's the reason you can see us. If you shout to your parents, we'll just disappear up the chimney."

"The chimney?" puzzled Lily. "Why the chimney?"

"Oh dear, this girl is not too smart," grumbled Billy. "Let's go."

"No, no, don't go!" yelled Lily, but the Watchers had gone in a blink of an eye.

The bedroom door burst open and Lily's mum rushed in. "What on earth's the matter?" she said. "I heard you shouting."

"Oh," mumbled Lily. "Sorry mum. I think I was dreaming. Sorry."

"O.K." said mum softly. "Lie down and go back to sleep. It will soon be morning."

Lily snuggled under her duvet. There was no sign or sound of the Watchers. She stared into the dark and before she knew it she was fast asleep.

Granny Green

Next morning Lily wondered if she should ask her mum, or dad, about 'Watchers'. If she wasn't careful they would become suspicious. They might think she was making up stories. Suppose they took her to the doctor, or, even worse, to see the headteacher. Her own teacher would be in trouble because the head teacher would think the teacher had been telling them strange stories. No. What she needed was to talk to her friends Max and Joe. Did they have Watchers or would they think she was mad?

Lily stirred her cornflakes round the bowl. Mum was putting a large sponge cake into a tin. Lily wondered why. Cakes usually went on a shelf in the cupboard. "What's the matter Lily?" asked mum. "You're very quiet this morning."

"Mum. I was just thinking. Have you ever heard of Watchers, you know, people who watch over you?"

"Yes," said mum as she put the cake tin in the middle of the table. "They are supposed to keep an eye on children, or sometimes adults, to make sure they are safe. In fact, some people think that they have an invisible Watcher sitting on their shoulder to watch over them. They sometimes call them Guardian Angels. Why do you want to know?"

"Oh, no reason, I just wanted to know."

"Was it something you were reading in a book?" puzzled mum.

"No," said Lily being careful as to what she said. She didn't want to tell lies. "There are people at school who think everyone has a Watcher, or Guardian Angel, like you said, one on each shoulder!"

"Well yes," agreed mum. "That's because it's part of their religion. It's what they believe in. That's what I meant when I said some people believe in them."

"Well, could you actually see a Guardian, I mean, Watcher, if you believed in them?"

"I don't know," said mum, "but sometimes I think I've got one, especially when something turns out right when there's trouble. A bit like when our Landlord turned us out of our old house and then let us move into this one."

"If you saw one, would you think you were dreaming?" continued Lily.

"I suppose so," said Mum. "Anyway, why all these questions about Watchers all of a sudden? Anything to do with that dream you had last night?"

"I suppose so," muttered Lily. "Just thought I'd ask – it doesn't matter."

"O.K. then," said mum. "Off you go out to play 'cos I'm busy. I've got to finish baking before I go to the shops."

Lily wandered into the street. Her two friends Max and Joe were sitting on the edge of the pavement outside Lily's house. They both lived in the same street as Lily. Joe lived next door and Max lived two doors down. All of them went to the same school; in fact they were all in the same class.

"Hi-ya Max, Hi-ya Joe. You playing?" asked Lily.

"Yeah," said Max, "but have you heard the news? We might not be able to live here soon."

"What do you mean?" asked Lily.

"I mean, we've got to move," answered Max.

"Yeah," joined in Joe. "I heard my mum and dad talking about it this morning."

"But we've only just moved here from the last house," said Lily. "How come?"

"It's that Landlord again," grumbled Max. "He's just mean and greedy. Now he's managed to clear people out of Green Street he's trying to move everyone from here too. He's given us all a few months to find somewhere else to live. That's the second time he's done this to us!"

"I don't want to move again," groaned Lily. "We could be miles away from each other."

"Or even be at a new school," groaned Max (who didn't much like school anyway).

"Yes," said Lily as she slipped her 'phone into her jean's pocket. "We'd have to make new friends and that can take ages."

"Hm!" agreed Joe, "and there's always someone who doesn't like you!"

The three friends went on muttering as they strolled down the street.

"I know!" said Lily suddenly. "Why don't we walk around the streets and see if there are any empty houses that our mums and dads might want to move into?"

"O.K." agreed Max, "but not far. We're not supposed to wander off!"

"Right!" said Lily as she pulled out her 'phone. "I'll send a text to mum and tell her what we're doing." She tapped in the message and pressed - SEND.

"Good idea," said Max. "We can go around and say hello to Granny Green too, in Green Street."

"Green Street?" interrupted Joe. "You mean where we used to live? I thought that those houses were all empty and isn't that the street where those lads were messing about?"

"Yes," continued Lily as her 'phone beeped to say she had received a message. "Granny Green is the only person left living in that street."

"How come?" asked Joe.

"Well, it's because she owns that house. She doesn't rent it like we do ours. She's refusing to move out."

Lily looked at the message on her 'phone. "Listen guys, mum says I can go if I take the cake she's made to Granny Green. Why don't you two go and tell your mums where we are going and I'll pick up the cake? I'll meet you at the end of the street in 10 minutes."

Ten minutes later the friends were on their way to Granny Green's house. It was in the next street, half way down. The whole street looked shabby and run down. Weeds were pushing up through the pavement cracks. Holes were in the road where the old cobblestones had been taken out. Most of the windows were boarded up, or smashed. But **not** Granny Green's house. It looked bright, clean and well cared for. The windows sparkled, the step was scrubbed clean and the letter box shone.

"I wonder how long she'll be able to live here before someone tries to move her?" wondered Max as he gazed around.

"I shall stay as long as I want," said a voice from the doorway, making him jump. "What do you want Young Man?"

Max turned to see an old woman staring at him. She was leaning on a stick which made her look a bit crooked and she seemed a little frail and – and – old. But, her eyes sparkled and a cheeky smile lit up her face.

"Err – err – we've come – come – to – err-,"

"What he's trying to say Granny Green, is that we've brought you a cake," explained Lily. "My mum made it this morning and said to bring it round whilst we explored."

"Ah, it's you Lily," said Granny Green "I thought I recognised that face. What a nice surprise. You tell your mum now that I said thank you. It is very welcome as I don't get to do much baking of my own nowadays. For a moment I thought you were those bad boys coming back to see what else they could take from my house."

"What do you mean Granny Green?" asked Max beginning to fell braver now that he knew the old lady wasn't going to shout at them.

"Granny Green? Hm!" repeated Granny Green. "I'm usually called Mrs Green, not Granny," she looked straight at Max and then smiled, "but I like it."

"Phew!" sighed Max.

"You see," continued Granny Green "those two boys were smashing windows and ran away before I could shout at them. Then, they came back last week and broke into my house whilst I was asleep. They must have heard me when I got out of bed because they banged the front door as they ran out."

"Wow!" exclaimed Lily. "Were you scared? Did they take anything?"

"I certainly WAS scared when I woke up and heard them, but they had gone by the time I got downstairs with my stick. They'd made a bit of a mess and they'd taken a vase and a few other things. The Police said the boys probably thought all the houses were empty and didn't notice in the dark that someone still lived here."

"That's stupid," said Joe. "How could they NOT notice? After all, the other houses have boarded windows."

"Yes," said Granny Green, "but I had left my door unlocked so they probably thought that this house hadn't yet been made secure. Still, I'll not forget to lock it from now on. Here, give me that cake before you drop it and I'll put it on the table inside."

Granny Green slowly climbed the two steps and disappeared into the house.

"Wow," said Max. "I bet that was scary for her."

"Yeah," said Joe. "Fancy being in a house on your own when there are burglars downstairs. It would be scary enough if you were with your mum and dad. I wonder if someone was looking out for Granny Green. It's to be hoped they don't come back again."

"Yes," agreed Joe. "Perhaps we should walk around here every day, just to check."

At that moment Granny Green appeared in the doorway.

"Now you three, take one of these sweets and Lily, don't forget to tell your mum thanks very much for the cake. Do you think you can collect the tin sometime?"

"Course I can," said Lily. "No prob - err - problem, I mean. We've just decided we'll walk around here sometimes to check on anyone who seems to be up to no good. They might come back you know."

"That's very good of you," said Granny Green, "although there's not much else of value to take."

"You mean what they took before was valuable?" gasped Max.

"I'm afraid so, Young Man," sighed Granny Green. "The vase they took was old and had belonged to my grandmother."

"That's not fair," grumbled Max. "People shouldn't steal, especially from old people. Not that YOU'RE old," he added, grinning.

"Not so much of the 'old', thank you," said Granny Green. "I can still throw up a sweet and catch it in my mouth," and with that she threw one of the sweets into the air, leaned back and neatly caught the sweet between her teeth.

"Wow!" muttered Max.

"Cool!" added Joe.

"Ace!" said Lily smiling.

"Funny though," puzzled Granny Green crunching the sweet slowly. "I'm not sure what really frightened them. Why did the front door suddenly bang so hard? It was almost as if someone was watching them, you know, like a watch dog or guard or something and frightened them away."

"Or a Guardian Watcher," muttered Lily.

"Yes," came back the reply. Granny Green had very good hearing despite being old. "Yes, just like a Guardian Watcher, or Guardian Angel as we used to call them when I was a little girl. A Watcher to keep me safe would be nice. Anyway off you go and play and keep a lookout for those boys. If you see any funny looking characters about, just let me know."

"O.K." they said together, waved and walked off down the street.

A Plan?

The three friends walked slowly away from Granny Green's.

"She's nice – for an old lady," said Max.

"Yeah, good trick that – catching that sweet," muttered Joe. "I have trouble catching a ball with my hands – never mind a sweet in the mouth!"

"She's cool," said Lily. "To think she came out of hospital not so long ago too. That's why she's got a stick to help her walk. Mum said she'd only been home a week when those boys broke in. That's probably why they thought the house was empty."

"Right," said Max. "No wonder they got a fright and ran away when the door slammed."

"But not before they'd taken some of her stuff," interrupted Joe. "Pity she doesn't have a Guardian Angel to watch over her." He stuck his hands in his pockets, thinking. "We should think of a way to help her."

"We could walk round the street each day," Suggested Max, "but we can't be there all the time."

Lily had been very quiet up to now.

"What do you think, Lil?" asked Joe.

"We-ell," started Lily, "you know what you said about Guardian Angels? Well, Granny Green must have one already. A Watcher, I mean."

"What are you talking about?" said Joe. "I was only joking you know. You're not going to tell me a load of stuff about fairies and magic, are you?" He stared at Lily. She'd stopped next to one of the empty houses, eyes down, looking at the pavement. Then, she sat down on the crumbling doorstep.

"Listen, you guys," she said quietly. "I'm going to tell you something that happened to me last night. I don't suppose you'll believe me, but here it is anyhow."

For the next five minutes the only sound to be heard in the street was the quiet sound of Lily's voice as she told the boys what had happened in her bedroom. She kept her eyes on the ground. She daren't look at them in case they were laughing at her. When she had finished she waited for the boys to tell her not to be so stupid, that it was a dream, a shadow, a noise from the street, something!

"Phew!" exclaimed Joe. "That's really - ."

"Cool!" gasped Max. "You really saw them – really?"

"Yep," said Lily looking up at the boys. Joseph and Max were both staring at her with large, round eyes.

"Crikey," said Joseph. "Does that mean we've – I've – got a Watcher too?"

"I should think so," said Lily, "but it seems you only see them if there's some sort of trouble happening – and of course – if you believe in them."

"Wow!" exclaimed the boys together.

Suddenly Joseph shouted, "That's it! That's how we can help Granny Green. We can ask the Watchers, especially **her** Watcher, to keep a look out for her – that's if she still has one."

"Oh yeah?" said Lily very sarcastically "And how do you suppose we do that then – shout a message into the air, send a text, email, write a letter? Have you any idea how we contact these Watchers, because I haven't?"

"Hm! Hadn't thought about that," muttered Joe.

"I know," said Max. "Let's see if your Watcher comes back tonight. You can tell her the problem and see what she says. Then we can take it from there and make plans."

All three nodded their heads. After a couple of high fives, Max came up with another idea.

"Let's check out the empty houses on each side of Granny Green's house and see if there are any clues as to why those boys are hanging around. We'll have to be careful though. In the first place the houses are not too safe, and second, my parents said not to go near them. Thirdly, those two boys might be around. One of us will have to keep watch in case they decide to come back whilst we're in there."

"Right," decided Lily. "Let's go!"

The friends headed for the first house next to Granny Green's. Max stayed outside whilst Joe and Lily looked around. After five minutes the two appeared at the doorway.

"Nothing in here," said Lily.

"Nope, just dust, cobwebs and spiders," said Joe.

"Yuk" muttered Max.

"Well, what do you expect?" Lily pointed out. "These houses have been empty for nearly 6 months. It's a pity someone has broken the windows as they were boarded up. They could be fixed into nice homes!"

"Not a chance," muttered Max. "Have you ever met the Landlord? He's just after clearing the site and making some money. He doesn't care about the people who lived here."

"Come on then," cut in Joe, getting bored. "Let's check another one and then we can go home. It must be dinner time soon and I'm getting hungry!"

"Here, have my sweet," said Lily. "It will keep you going for a while."

She and Joe checked another house and then they went back to the one on the other side of Granny Green's.

"Look," whispered Lily as they went into the hallway, "this staircase is still O.K. Let's go up and look around."

They tip-toed carefully across the small landing at the top of the stairs. A quick glance told them that the rooms up here were empty and not in very good repair. At the end of the landing they noticed a little door in the wall. Joe pulled it open.

"Look Lily, there's another narrow staircase here. Looks like it goes up to the roof."

"Nah," said Lily. "It goes to the attic. It's just like the house we used to live in. Shall we go up?"

"Yeah," said Joe, "but let me go first 'cos I've got my torch with me."

In the attic it took a while for their eyes to accustom to the dark shapes around them. Joe shone his torch around the room.

"Ouch!" moaned Lily as she tripped over something in the gloom.

"What's up?" asked Joe.

"Something I fell over," muttered Lily as she rubbed her knees. She'd caught them on something rough. Joe shone his torch to where he could see the faint outline of Lily.

"Be careful," he warned her. "You had me scared there for a minute. Say, what's that you're sitting next to?"

Lily turned towards the shaft of light shining from the torch onto the ground. An old curtain covered something round and bulky right next to where she had stumbled. Next to it were some cardboard boxes. Crumpled newspapers were sticking out of each box.

"Strange," wondered Joe. "Surely these houses should be empty?"

"Perhaps they're things they didn't want," puzzled Lilly. "Do you think we should have a look?"

"Don't suppose it will do any harm," he said "as long as we're careful and don't break anything – just in case".

"Wow!"

Lily was already pulling off the old curtain from the lumpy shape next to her.

"It's an old jar, look!"

Joe shone his torch closer.

"It's a bit big for a flower vase," he remarked. "Don't think my mother would want it. In fact I think she would have left it behind too, it if was hers. It's yuk!"

"Oh you!" muttered Lily. "Can't you see? It's one of those large old Chinese vases. See, it has pictures of dragons and people all over it – and look, strange writing on it too."

"Hm? It's all Chinese to me," murmured Joe, trying to be funny.

Lily ignored him and lifted the lid on the top of the vase. She peered inside.

"Heck," she gasped. "It's full of money!"

"Money! Are we rich?" asked Joe.

"Don't be stupid," answered Lily. "We couldn't keep it if we wanted to. We should really take it to the Police."

"They wouldn't believe us though," added Joe. "They'd say we'd stolen it."

"Well then," decided Lily. "We'll have to try and get them to come here."

Whilst the two friends thought about this, a scuffle of feet sounded on the stairs.

"Hey, you two!" whispered a voice. It was Max.

"Quick, there's a couple of guys coming up the street!"

Lily pulled the curtain back over the vase and the three of them ran downstairs.

"Too late," said Max. "They'll see us coming out of the house."

"Now what?" exclaimed Joe.

"Shh!" ordered Lily. "Keep quiet. If they come in here, then it will be to check the things we just found. Listen, I remember there was a big cupboard in the bedroom right next to the door that led up to the attic. Let's hide in there."

The three ran back to the bedroom and found the cupboard.

"Yes!" whispered Lily. "Just as I thought. It's big enough for all three of us. Come on!"

As they closed the door of the cupboard behind them they heard footsteps and voices on the stairs.

"Come on," growled one voice. "Let's check the stuff. I saw some nosey kids around here a while ago. I want to make sure they haven't been in."

Heavy feet trod the stairs right up to the attic.

"Careful," said one voice, "It's a bit dark up here and my torch isn't very powerful."

"Is the stuff all there?" said another voice.

"Yes, we just have to get the Boss up here now so he can get rid of it for us. It should mean a nice pocketful of money for us to spend. Come on, let's go and find him and see what he says."

"What if he doesn't want the stuff?" asked the second voice.

"He will," answered the first voice. "He's done this before. He takes it to a friend of his who sells it. We have to do a deal. Come on, and don't fall down the stairs like you did last time!"

"As if!" said the second voice.

The friends held their breath. After a few minutes of silence Lily carefully pushed open the cupboard door. There was no sign or sound of the boys. They all climbed out, slipped downstairs and out onto the street. It was empty.

"Guess what!" sneezed Max as he dusted down his jacket. "I know those voices."

"You do?" gasped Joe.

"Mm," continued Max. "It's Lee and Len. They've just left school. They were always in trouble at school – thieving people's stuff and that. I heard they don't have jobs so they just mooch around making trouble and stealing things."

"Right!" decided Lily. "Here's what we do!"

Getting Help

That night Lily told her mum and dad she was tired and went to bed early. As soon as it grew darker she sat up in bed and waited. She knew mum and dad had gone to bed because there was no light shining under her bedroom door. All was quiet. She waited, and waited. Just as her eyelids were beginning to droop she suddenly heard a tiny 'shushing' noise near the fireplace. Then, a little voice whispered,

"What are we going to do if she's fast asleep?"

Lily saw six bright eyes staring straight at her.

"Hello," she whispered. "I'm glad you came back. Don't be afraid. I won't shout out like last time. I need to ask you something."

The six eyes disappeared. There was a flutter of wings and a shuffle of feet and soft whispers. Then, just as she had given up hope the six eyes suddenly reappeared right in front of her on the duvet. The three small Watchers looked straight at her. One of them was having trouble with his cap. It kept falling over his eyes.

"That's Sammy Sunshine," thought Lily. "I remember him from last time, and there's Billy, Billy Blue Wings."

Next to Billy was Rosy Red Wings. She was supposed to be Lily's Watcher.

"I'm glad you've come back again," said Lily out loud. "I've been talking to my friends Joe and Max. I told them about you."

"That's good," smiled Rosy. "That means you believe in us. Now we'll be able to stay."

"What do you mean?" asked Lily.

"Unless you believe in us," replied Rosy, "we are out of a job and would have to go away. Now, Sammy and Billy can visit Max and Joe."

"Wow!" gasped Lily. "That's really cool. They were hoping that they had a Watcher. In fact they are both sitting up in their bedrooms tonight waiting for you to appear."

"Yes!!" said Billy and Sammy together giving each other a 'high-five' and then spinning round in circles.

"O.K." said Rosy suddenly. "You two can go for a visit when we've finished here. Now, why were you waiting for us Lily? What did you want to know?"

Lily told the three Watchers all about the discovery they had made next door to Granny Green's house.

"Granny Green," pondered Billy, "Isn't that Gordon Green's lady? Isn't he the old Watcher who looks after her – and-,"

"Yes," cut in Sammy. "You remember, he was told off by the Supervisor for falling asleep when he was on guard duty. He got sent away for a short time."

"Oh," puzzled Lily. "I wonder if that was when Lee and Len took the stuff from Granny Green's house."

Lily finished telling them about the things in the attic. "So you see, we need to know what to do. Can you help?"

Rosy thought about what Lily had said. "Well," she replied. "Our Supervisor can't help at the moment because he's too busy, but he told us to visit our people and tell them what to do."

"Yes," interrupted Lily, "but what DO we do?"

"I suppose the first thing to try is to tell your parents," said Rosy looking at Sammy and Billy for support.

"Mm, yes," said Sammy. "We might be your Watchers and try to keep you safe, but we can't help as much as grown-ups can."

"That's all very well," said Lily, but how can I tell my parents about the stuff in the attic when I'm not supposed to go there. I'll get into awful trouble."

"Hmm," muttered Billy.

"Yes," agreed Rosy.

"Certainly will," added Sammy.

"I know what," said Billy suddenly (he was always full of bright ideas). "Tell your mum that you've seen someone lingering around at the end of the street and that you're worried about Granny Green."

"Great idea," smiled Rosy, "and if your parents don't help, then go and tell the Police.

Lily pulled the duvet up over her arms to keep warm and when she looked up again, the Watchers had gone.

Caught

Next morning after Lily had eaten her breakfast she spoke to her mum, just as the Watchers had suggested.

"Do you think those boys were the burglars mum?" she asked. "Do you think they were the ones who broke into Granny Green's house?"

"How do you know about that?" asked mum, stopping what she was doing and looking straight at Lily.

Lily fiddled with the knife and fork on her plate.

"Not sure," she muttered. "Probably Granny Green said something when we took her the cake."

"Well, don't you go messing around with anyone around that street. Today you can help me by taking these buns to Granny Green. You can collect the cake tin whilst you are there. Here you are. You could go now and then play out until dinner time because I've got to slip to the shops."

Lily took the bag of buns and shot out of the door before mum could ask her any more awkward questions. It didn't look as if mum was going to believe her. Max and Joe were already outside and she could see that they were really excited.

"What's up?" asked Lily.

Max and Joe were jumping up and down.

"We saw them, both of us," said Max. "We actually saw the Watchers. At least, we each saw our own and they were really cool. They told us your Guardian, Rosy, had had a word with you about Lee and Len."

"Yes, she did," said Lily, "but when I told mum about the boys, she just told me not to go near them. I don't know what to do next. I can't go and tell the Police. Mum would find out where I'd been."

Max and Joe stuck their hands in their pockets and they all started to walk to the end of the street.

"Look," said Lily suddenly, "I've got to take these buns to Granny Green and collect the cake tin, so why don't we check the house and make sure the stuff is still there in the attic?"

"Good idea," said Joe. "Then we can decide what to do next."

There was no answer when Lily knocked on Granny Green's door.

"She must have gone to the shop," decided Joe. "Why don't you leave the bag of buns on the doorstep whilst we have a look next door?"

Lily put down the bag of buns and they moved to the empty house. As they reached the landing with the attic door Lily remembered something.

"We forgot about a look-out. You two go up and check and I'll go out and watch."

The boys continued up the narrow attic stairs. Rosy walked carefully down the dark staircase and out of the door.

There, standing next to Granny Green's doorstep, with the last of the buns going into their mouths, were Lee and Len!

"Hey!" shouted Lily. "What are you doing with those buns? I brought them for Granny Green."

"What are YOU doing in that house?" snarled Lee. He took a step towards Lily.

Lily ran. She ran like the wind. She ran as if a pack of wild dogs were chasing her. When she reached the end of the street and glanced back there was no one following her.

All she could see were two legs sticking out from the steps of the empty house. She moved into the doorway of the last house on the street from where she could keep a look-out down the street. What was she going to do now? She hadn't had time to warn the boys. What was going on in that house? Would Lee and Len catch Max and Joe before they could escape?

After a while Lily saw the two boys emerging from the empty house. There was a slight argument, which Lily couldn't hear properly, and then they took off down the street, away from Lily. As soon as they turned the corner, Lily ran as fast as she could to the empty house.

"Max! Joe!" she shouted, but there was no reply.

The door was shut. She grabbed the door knob and turned it round. The door was locked!

"Oh no!" she panicked. "What do I do now?"

Suddenly she heard a little voice in her ear. "Go and tell your mum. We will stay with Max and Joe until you come back."

Lily knew straight away that it was Rosy Red Wings.

"So that's why people have Watchers," she thought as she ran away. "I wish I had my 'phone." But her 'phone was somewhere in the kitchen. She'd been in such a hurry to get away from mum and speak to Max and Joe that she'd forgotten to pick it up.

"Mum! Mum!" she shouted as she banged on the back door. "Where are you?"

There was no answer. The house was empty. What should she do now? No good going to school because it was closed for the holiday. The Police Station was a long way away and she would need a grown-up with her. She needed help, NOW! She couldn't leave her friends locked up in that dark house. She decided to go back and see if there was any way she could get through the door.

It seemed to take her ages to get there. She could hardly catch her breath and her legs ached. She skidded to a stop at the door of the empty house. The door was old with peeling paint, but it was still a very strong door. No matter how she pulled and pushed, it wouldn't move. What now?

"What do you think you are doing?" said a voice behind her.

Lily froze. Had Lee and Len returned? Slowly, she turned around. It was Granny Green! Rosy let out a sigh of relief.

"Oh Granny Green!" she exclaimed. "We must get help."

"Why, what on Earth's the matter?" asked Granny Green, looking puzzled, but concerned. "Come inside and tell me."

She opened her door and went in. Lily didn't want to leave the empty house, but she followed her. As Granny Green sat herself down on a chair, Lily told her everything that had happened.

"And I'm going to get into awful trouble when mum and dad find out," she groaned.

"Right," said Granny Green. "You say the boys are locked in there?"

"Yes," said Lily, "and it'll be dark soon, and we're not supposed to be going into those houses, and we're going to be in trouble, and I don't know what to do!" Lily was close to tears. She rubbed her eyes and looked at Granny Green.

"Come on," said Granny Green, standing up. "We're going to the Police Station, right now."

"But my mum?" trembled Lily.

"Leave your mum to me," said Granny Green.

She locked the door and they set off towards the Police Station. Lily took one last look up at the empty house and wondered if she'd see her friends again.

Max and Joseph

Inside the empty house it was pitch black except for a chink of light coming through a small hole in the roof. Max and Joe had heard Lily rattling the front door. They'd heard her shouting, but then she had gone away. Did she realise that they were still up here, or did she think they had managed to get out of the house when Lee and Len appeared?

If she did think they had got away, it would be a long time before anyone would realise that they had disappeared. They were trapped and they were scared. What would Lee and Len do when they came back? The boys had been really angry when they came up the stairs and found them there. It had been too dark to make a dash for it, and anyway Len had blocked the narrow staircase with his body. What was it they had said as they left - - - - "We'd better get the Landlord here. He'll know what to do."

"Oh no! thought Max. "We're really in trouble if that nasty Landlord comes."

He tried to stretch out his legs. They were aching from sitting in this cramped position, but the strips of curtain around his ankles were making it difficult to move. He couldn't move his hands either. They were tied and there was a horrible rag wrapped around his mouth so that he couldn't shout out or talk to Joe. He knew Joe was sitting there next to him. Their shoulders were touching. At least he wasn't on his own.

Then he noticed something in the chink of light shining on the floor. Two sets of eyes had suddenly appeared. It was their Watchers, Billy and Sammy.

"Don't worry," said Billy. "You'll be O.K. Rosy has sent Lily to get help."

"Yes," said Sammy. "I'm afraid we're too small to untie you, but we'll be here keeping watch over you."

As Max and Joe blinked their eyes, the two Watchers disappeared.

The Police Station

At the Police Station Lily was having trouble getting the Sergeant to believe her.

"Are you reporting someone missing?" he enquired.

"No. No. I keep telling you. Max and Joe are not missing; they've been locked in an empty house."

"How do you know this then?" he asked.

"Because I was there when they went in," she replied.

"So YOU locked the door then?"

"No! I ran away."

'Ran away' wrote the Sergeant in his notebook.

"So you shut the door and ran away."

"No!" shouted Lily, just about in tears by now.

"Now then," said the Sergeant softly. "No need to shout at me. However, if you are playing tricks you'd better go home and stop wasting my time."

"Young man," said a voice behind Lily. "I think you had better listen to what this young lady has to tell you."

The Sergeant looked at Granny Green. He looked at Lily.

"Go in there," he said pointing to a door. "Sit down and I'll be with you in a second."

"They don't believe me," said Lily getting agitated as she sat down on a chair. "What are we going to do?"

"Don't worry," said Granny Green patting her on the back. "Just tell the truth."

When the Sergeant came in with his notebook and pencil Lily told him the whole story. As she stopped he leaned back in his chair and looked at Granny Green.

"Do you think this girl is telling the truth?" he asked.

"Of course," said Granny Green. "You know all about these boys, Lee and Len. I've reported them to you more than once."

"Yes," realised the Sergeant. "I thought I had seen you before. Look. I'll send a couple of my police constables over there to look around and see what happens. How about that Lily?"

"Right now?" asked Lily.

"Right now," said the Sergeant. "If Lee and Len have locked up your friends then we can take further action. Granny Green, can you take Lily home and explain things to her parents and then tell Max and Joseph's parents?"

"Of course I can," agreed Granny Green as she followed Lily out of the door.

Two police constables were already driving away in a police car towards Green Street.

As she had suspected Lily's parents were not too pleased with her when Granny Green told them the story, but they were relieved to know that at least SHE was safe. Her dad went straight round to Max and Joe's houses and brought back their parents to Lily's house. A long conversation took place about what they should do next. Finally, Lily's dad, Max's dad and Joseph's dad decided to go around to the empty house to see if they could help.

Granny Green, Lily's mum, Max and Joe's mum and Lily all sat down around the kitchen table. None of them touched the mugs of tea that Lily's mum had made. They didn't even talk. Five minutes went by, then half an hour, then a full hour passed by.

"Why are you looking so pleased with yourself?" asked Lily's mum looking straight at her.

"Because I know everything is going to be O.K." smiled Lily. "We all have Watchers looking after us, so I know the boys will be O.K."

"Let's hope so," said mum.

Granny Green and Lily looked at each other. Granny Green winked. She knew, and so did Lily.

"Now then," said mum. "Tonight you must stay with us Granny Green until we find out what is happening."

"Yes," agreed Granny Green. "I suppose I'd better stay here and be safe until the Police have sorted out everything."

The Landlord

"What on earth did you think you were doing? I told you not to keep coming round here once you'd hidden the stolen goods!"

The Landlord was not pleased. In fact, he was very angry and trying hard not to shout.

"We were just checking," said Len. "You know, just to make sure everything was still there."

"Yeah," said Lee. "Those kids had been snooping around. We thought they'd find something."

"Well, they did," said the Landlord. "Why on earth didn't you just frighten them away?"

"Because - - -," started Len.

"Oh, never mind," said the Landlord. "Let's get everything out of here. We'll put it in another house and then leave the door of this house unlocked so that those kids can be found."

The Landlord disappeared into the next house to check for a hiding place whilst Lee and Len brought out the stolen goods. When the Landlord had shown them where to hide everything, they left the house and walked straight into the arms of the waiting police!

"We'd like a word with you three," said the police constable, as the other constable who had come with him put handcuffs on them all.

"Listen," said the Landlord trying very hard not to look worried. "It has nothing to do with me. I just found these two in one of my houses. I think they've been stealing and hiding the goods in this house."

Lee and Len couldn't believe their ears! The Landlord was blaming them for everything.

"Don't bother trying to explain," smirked the police constable. "We have it on good authority that you were overheard making plans."

"Who says?" snarled the Landlord.

"We do," answered two voices, "and you're also guilty of kidnapping."

Max and Joe stumbled out of the empty house rubbing their eyes, mouths and wrists. They were followed by their rather dusty dads who had found them in the attic.

"Right," said the constable to his colleague. "Put these three in the car and take them to the station to be questioned. You two and your dads come with me. I think your mums will be very pleased to see you again."

Rewards

That night, after mum had tucked her in, Rosy sat upright in bed waiting for the dark to arrive. As the first beams of moonlight shone through the crack in the curtains, two little eyes appeared at the foot of the bed.

"Hello Rosy," whispered Lily. "I've been waiting for you so I can tell you what happened.

"Sorry," said Rosy, "I had to go to the Supervisor and report on what was going on. That's why I'm late. He told Billy and Sammy and me to go back to our children and make sure they were O.K."

"We're fine," said Lily. "The police caught Lee and Len and the Landlord. They say they will be in prison for quite some time. Max and Joe are O.K. Billy Blue Wings and Sammy Sunshine helped them to be brave whilst they were tied up in the house and Granny Green has all her things back safe and sound." Rosy stopped for a breath before she continued, "Guess what? The Police

Sergeant said the old vase was worth a small fortune. Apparently it's very rare, and if Granny Green puts it up for auction, she could get thousands and thousands of pounds for it."

"Fantastic! That sounds good," said Rosy who didn't know much about money. "I hope that doesn't mean she's going to move away somewhere. Gordon Green Wings wouldn't be able to get a new person to watch. He's getting old. He wants to stay with Granny Green."

"No, that's the best part," said Lily excitedly. "Granny Green says she's going to buy the houses in her street from the Landlord with the money from the auction. She's going to let us all move back into Green Street and we only have to pay a small rent to stay there."

"That's good," said Rosy, smiling. "Well I'd better be off and see if the boys have told Sammy and Billy the good news."

"Can I give you something, a present I mean, to say thank you for helping us?" asked Lily.

"You already have," said Rosy. "The Supervisor is so pleased with us for helping you to stay brave and sort out things that he's given us a medal. If we collect three medals, we get new wings!"

"Wow!" said Lily. "What do you have to do to get more medals?"

"Just wait and see," smiled Rosy and as Lily blinked, Rosy disappeared.